D1605922

It All Came Tumbling Down

Considerations on How to Deal with Grief, Trauma and Loss

Library of Congress Cataloging-in-Publication Data Name: Howard, Valerie Overton

Title: It All Came Tumbling Down, Considerations on How to Deal with Grief, Trauma and Loss

ISBN 9798419292024

Published by GHW Productions LLC 2019
Cunningham Dr., Ste. 416
Hampton, VA 23666   www.manifestdestinyllc3.com

Because of the Internet's dynamic nature, any web addresses or links contained in this book may have changed since publication and may no longer be valid. The views expressed in this work are solely those of the author and do not necessarily reflect the publisher's views, and the publisher hereby disclaims any responsibility for them.

Acknowledgments

My Spiritual Father is my EVERYTHING. I am so grateful to have a STRONG village of individuals who have walked alongside me during various stages in my life. I strive to show my gratitude and express my love frequently. Without my parents, Rose and David Dower, I would not be the woman I am today.

They fortified me with spiritual awareness, loyalty, morals, determination, kindness, direction, and understanding of the importance of family and being a woman of my word.

My grandmother Elizabeth Overton was our pillar and the epitome of love. This is why I named an organization after her, The Love of Elizabeth.

Growing up for me came with a lot of unexpected challenges. But I received foundational teachings from my amazing Godparents, Kelly and Darlene Grandison, my mentor Glenda Johnson, encourager Pastor Dianna Bruno, Mamma Girt, big sister Mildred Taylor Houston and youth ministers Tommy and Minnie West (who learned to cook while trying out her recipes on us innocent young people; she pinched us too!) along with my loyal best friends Tracey Williams and little sister Angela Overton for over 25 years.

I have been blessed with unbelievable support from my brothers, especially David and William Overton, (God rest his soul.) family members, my pastors Elder Robert and Lady Jean Burroughs, and Elder Willis and Lady Betty

Williams. Along with my God-brothers, ALL OF MY AWESOME MOTHER FIGURES, youth ministers, mentors, teachers, seasoned saints, my treasured friendships, my church family, and a host of individuals who have been instrumental during transitional journeys in my life.

Charles Howard has been a perfect role model demonstrating undying strength and perseverance. Thank you for blossoming into the man God created to love me. Micah Charlton Jr. and Alice Howard have endured unwarranted pain and devastating circumstances that could have destroyed them, but my babies are continually plowing towards their purpose and destiny. So proud of you both! Thank you, Aunt Fay, for being there for me and stepping up when Mother Rose left this earth.

I would like to thank Counselor Mathis for partnering with me to orchestrate and execute annual mental health workshops and events for families and community members. I appreciate you for supporting me and believing in my visions.

Disclaimer

This book's information and recommendations are the author's personal experiences, points of view, and options to consider for individuals going through grief, trauma, and loss. People have different experiences, thus responding differently to the absence of a person, entity, place, or thing.

The intent of the author is to offer her personal experiences stemming from her pain, loss, and trauma. The author is not professing to be a trained professional. However, as a certified Success Coach, the author presents powerful questions and opportunities to consider and select diverse options. The goal is to have an authentic conversation with the reader.

This book is not a substitute for medical treatment or advice from a skilled professional. Nor is it suggesting the discontinuation of treatment, therapy, or prescribed medications.

Any application of the suggestions expounded upon for consideration is undertaken at your own risk. The author disclaims all liability in connection with the use of the information, ideas to be considered, or suggestions presented.

It All Came Tumbling Down

Considerations on How to Deal
with Grief, Trauma, and Loss

IMPORTANT INFORMATION: If at any time while reading this book you are compelled to speak to someone, or you are feeling hopeless, please call 1-800-888-6161 or text Hope to 741741, (United States) available 24 hours, seven days a week. I want you to know you are not alone, and regardless of what you are going through or have been through, there is light at the end of the tunnel. You are brave, and I believe in your recovery process. You deserve to live your best life. Your pain may be before you, but you have a bright future ahead of you. I am here with you to embrace your fears, face your tears and look forward to productive years. Let's begin your journey so you can heal from the inside out.

Table of Contents

Be Strong

Standing over the coffin was a man grieving, tears dripping down his face, while he viewed the lifeless body of his only biological son who bore his name. He was heartbroken and devastated because his 17-year-old son's life was stolen from him, murdered by the hands of a "friend." In that moment of devastation, before closing the casket, he was faced with the unbearable feeling of knowing it would be the last time he would ever lay eyes upon his *golden child.* Then, as he held the lid of the casket in his hand, proclaiming his final farewell, a gentleman touched his shoulder slightly and whispered, "Be strong, don't let the people see you cry." At that very moment, I had to eradicate that statement, dismissing the myth that men shouldn't cry and sending reassurance that it was ok to embrace the emotion and release it. So instead, I simply said this three-letter word, "Cry."

During that sobering incident, it was evident that traditions and how people were raised can affect how they deal with grief, trauma, or loss. After taking a class at Cleveland State University about Black Issues in America, I was enlightened and educated concerning the struggles of African Americans. Some customs and unspoken norms are still woven within some families' fibers.   The impact and trauma of slavery have influenced how African Americans progress or digress in their lives. This book will not highlight black history or racial disparities. Still, it is imperative to point out how the past can affect how we approach circumstances or how strongholds can instigate generational behaviors.

Travel with me back in time. Can you imagine a man of color having an emotional meltdown and bursting into tears while being stripped of his family and sold into slavery? As I pondered the question, I began to analyze the idea that he would have had to represent strength because he wasn't viewed as a man but as an object, a piece of property. Property? Yes! That idea is still a norm in some workplaces, political arenas, educational institutions, and even some homes. Some parents view their children or family members as their entity or belonging. They may want their children or family to possess an unstoppable strength or demonstrate a demeanor of durability, but definitely not a weakness or frailty. Stereotypically in the past, men wanted their sons to represent strength, so that is why I immediately dismissed the possible notion of men not being able to express the pain inside due to what was taught.

When I reflect on the gentleman's comment during such a befitting time to express an emotional outcry, I wonder what he was taught or what norm he was mirroring while standing at the coffin.

What restraints have you experienced when attempting to or expressing your emotions?

_____

_____

_____

_____

_____

_____

_____

_____

_____

_____

_____

_____

What is your family norm about openly expressing emotions? Give an example of this that you recall?

_____

_____

_____

_____

_____

_____

_____

_____

_____

_____

I appreciate when people tell me how strong I am, but I remind them that I am human and feel the pain most individuals feel. For example, if you cut me, I will bleed.

Can you elaborate on when you wanted to express emotion but felt like you had to be strong for someone?

_____
_____
_____
_____

Who or what did you have to be strong for during the incident you described?

_____
_____
_____
_____
_____
_____
_____
_____

Empty Inside

Losing someone or something dear to you can trigger a plethora of emotions you never knew existed or put you in a state of disbelief or even denial. After a loss or trauma, I have heard people describe feeling loss analogically by referring to a hole in their heart, a void, a hollow place, an indescribable pain, or the feeling of desperation, vulnerability, or devastation.

Can you recall one time when you lost someone or something? (Please allow yourself to feel this for a moment. If it is not possible right now, please refer to this question later)

_____

_____

_____

_____

_____

_____

_____

_____

What is the first thing that came to your mind as you began to reminisce?

_____

_____

_____

_____

_____

_____

_____

_____

_____

What did you feel when you lost the person or the thing?

_____

_____

_____

_____

_____

_____

_____

_____

Acute stress disorder (ASD, also known as an acute stress reaction, psychological shock, mental shock, or simply shock) is a psychological response to a terrifying, traumatic, or surprising experience.

I remember the first traumatic experience I had during the loss of my covenant son. At certain times, I felt like I could not think, I was forgetful, and my memory and thought pattern seemed sporadic. I could not connect the dots, and certain things seemed cloudy. At first, I thought I was losing my mind or having early signs of dementia because I couldn't remember things, and I was not as sharp or on point.

Have you ever had a pencil break? In most cases, you don't throw away the pencil. You either sharpen it or push it up if it is a mechanical pencil. If you can relate, try not to panic because counseling, time, mental health techniques, exercise, or medication can aid in helping you sharpen the points or areas in your life that have been broken.

Can you think of a time when you felt like you were disconnected? If so, can you elaborate?

_____
_____
_____
_____
_____
_____
_____
_____

Before losing my covenant son, I could slice through my thoughts, have creative come-back answers, and reply strategically and meaningfully. But at one point, I had to take time to think and gather my thoughts. It felt like things were scattered and all over the place. It felt like my thoughts were floating in the air, and I couldn't reach them—fireflies in the night.

Grabbing for answers, grasping for my next breath, and wondering what I did to deserve such pain became a constant part of my daily mental routine of thoughts and questions.

I was swamped with emotions and a list of unending questions. Why was I being emptied? Why was I being gutted? Why was my heart pulled out of my chest? Why was my soul being poured out?

Can you elaborate on when you felt some of the emotions I expressed in the paragraph above?

_____
_____
_____
_____
_____
_____
_____
_____

Have you dealt with how you felt? If so, what have you done to deal with it?

_____
_____
_____
_____
_____
_____
_____
_____
_____
_____
_____

Bitter vs. Sweet

If you have experienced losing a child, have you ever looked around and observed people with their children? Have you observed individuals purchasing Mother, Father, Grandparents, Valentine's Day, or other memorable occasional day cards/gifts, and you have no parents to visit or individuals to celebrate? Have you seen people advance on their job, and you were fired? Or have you seen people pass you up and take your position while you were being demoted? What about seeing women have babies who didn't want them, and you are infertile—seeing married couples sharing intimate gestures and recently losing your spouse—watching people dance and you have no limbs? Or anything else that made you feel bitter?

Write an encounter such as this that you experienced?

_____
_____
_____
_____
_____
_____
_____
_____

How did you overcome these feelings, or are you still working through them?

_____

_____

_____

_____

_____

_____

_____

_____

If you have not overcome them, how do you deal with them? (Example - by ignoring it or self-medicating. Remember, this is your book and your experiences, so you can be totally honest.)

_____

_____

_____

_____

_____

_____

_____

_____

_____

Our daughter, Alice, was several months old when her father placed a lemon in her mouth. Immediately she reacted to the sour taste, turned her head, made a funny face, and tried to rid the aftertaste off her tongue and lips. Poor Alice. Her father constantly introduced her palate to something her tiny body had never experienced. So she was given something sweet in the subsequent encounter and responded with a smile and desired more.

When trauma or loss hits our life, we react. Usually, it feels sour and bitter. I have never desired or requested more pain. I wanted it to stop. It didn't feel sweet or compelling; it felt unbearable. We must monitor our hearts not to become bitter and full of rage or hate in times like this. If we don't get the help we need, we can react to the situation resentfully or unpleasantly, affecting our relationships, home life, work performance, and how we function.

How did you respond when trauma or loss hit your life?

_____

_____

_____

_____

_____

_____

_____

_____

What did it squeeze out of you? Bitterness, anger, and confusion, all the above or *something else*?

_____

_____

_____

_____

_____

_____

_____

_____

_____

If you squeeze a lemon, bitter juice will come out of it, but it can embody sweetness if a saccharine additive is incorporated. We can do the same thing with our life and add sweet memories.

Someone may have a signature drink at a party or special event. Being whimsical, they may give the drink a name. I created a drink mixture called "Valerie's New Chapter during my trauma." I took my trauma mixed with a spiritual agave to create inner healing. Mix the pain with sweet moments, stir hurt with the desire to advance, and intertwine despair with hope. My grandmother always used to say, "Turn those lemons into lemonade."

What does your mixture look like, and what would you name it?

_____

_____

_____

_____

_____

_____

_____

There may be a pessimistic force sitting on your shoulder trying to influence you to think life won't or can't get any better. I encourage you to dust it off and embrace hope and optimism. Mix your purpose and positivity, and you will have some good old sweet lemonade or a hopeful outlook on life. Put your feet up, sit in the sun, watch the sunset, and know that the sun will rise again in the morning.

A Pot, Colander –
Strainer of Emotions

What are you holding your emotions in? A pot, colander, or strainer? What is a colander? What is the difference between a colander and a strainer?

A strainer is a catchall name for any type of, well -- strainer. It is usually fine mesh and bowl-shaped. It is good for rinsing a pint of berries or draining pasta. When straining items, you are careful to avoid anything from slipping through. Have you ever tried to drain something and lost most of it while pouring it out? I remember when I drained spaghetti in the wrong pot, most of the noodles went right down the drain!

During your loss, grief or trauma, be careful to ensure that you don't lose who you are in the process of draining. It can be a little challenging to rid yourself of what is inside without losing who you are. For example, some may have lost their spouse or people you were around daily or often. However, being with these individuals and practicing specific rituals or customs can become a part of who you are, and it is hard to see yourself without them.

Trying to drain an item without the proper strainer can be challenging. Another draining receptacle is a colander. Typically, a larger bowl-shaped strainer that often has bigger holes. If you tried to drain rice in this type of pot, it would result in your rice going down the drain.

The thought of existing without who or what you lost can be unimaginable. Suppose you can visualize draining your trauma or grief, not the person or the event out of your life. While doing this, don't allow your dreams and goals to slip out of the colander and go down the drain with your loss. Don't let what you've lost make you feel lost, lose your desire to live, or lose your ambitions and aspirations. You can still be creative, anointed, smart, important, significant, and reach the finish line.

If you keep all your emotions in a pot, that is where they will be contained. When you put water in a pot and turn on the stove without tending to it, it will eventually boil over. When we keep our emotions on the inside unattended, anger may boil over and potentially burn or scald those nearby. The saying is, "hurt people hurt people." Not everyone intends to cause pain to those in the vicinity, but it can happen. Although it is time for the griever to grieve, try not to form a barrier or injure those who care for you during the process. If you have noticed yourself doing that, it may be essential to reflect if you are full of what's in your pot and begin to release the pain. You may ask how. Drain it. How do I drain it? You can start by talking to your higher power, someone you trust, or journaling about your pain. We will provide other techniques to consider later in the book. These suggestions may help you drain some of the pain, but remember to use the right strainer to hold back all that is worth holding on to.

I tell people that you may get burned if you touch the pot when it is too hot. However, not everyone is out to get you. Some people are nosy; some don't care, but don't burn those who want to touch/help you. Simply ask the person to give you a little time and space if needed and reaffirm your love and appreciation for them. It's ok to take time to process, but I have found it beneficial to briefly let those close to you know you are trying to deal with "what's in your pot" called life. Sometimes, you may feel anger, but remember, anger hides behind other emotions; what are you feeling?

What is on the inside of your pot?

_____
_____
_____
_____
_____

What are some of the dreams or ambitions you allowed to go down the drain?

_____
_____
_____
_____
_____
_____
_____
_____

Who can you talk to in order to help you drain?

_____

_____

Is there any individual(s) who got too close to your pot when it was hot?

_____

_____

_____

Would you be willing to let them know you appreciate them but that you need a little space for your emotions to cool down?

_____

Letting it Out

Have you ever had a balloon and wanted to let the air out? It will either make a noise or fly away fast all over the place. That is why it is good to let the air out little by little. Sometimes a person can be full of air, full of grief, full of distress, full of anger, or full of hurt. If you let it out too abruptly all at once, you may fly all over the place, but you can get a release and strategically rid yourself of the emotions if you let it out slowly.

I had experienced times when I sighed at the thought of what I was going through, and I felt a little better. It provided an avenue to let some air out and release some pockets of reactions. Letting air out of a balloon little by little is a form of letting go. A person can experience the same thing.

Take a deep breath and exhale. This is an exercise and will let some of the air out. When experiencing trauma, it is good to let how it has affected us out. Some people scream, dance, sing or simply cry. As mentioned before, talking to someone, exercising, or finding a positive way is another way of letting it go. We are not letting the person or thing go, but what we are feeling.

Please note, if it is an actual breakup or divorce, letting go of the person and the pain simultaneously may help you move on, especially if the other person has moved on.

Exercise: Right now, take a deep breath. Relax for a moment. Feel yourself letting it go.

How do you feel after taking a deep breath?

_____

_____

_____

_____

Psalm 121:1 states, *"I will lift up mine eyes unto the hills, from whence cometh my help,"* Indicating a focal point that provided assistance, comfort, support, and relief. After reading that, I view the hills as an object that took the place of the pain or trauma. When I took Lamaze class, they taught us to create a focal point to zoom in on something other than the pain when a contraction came.

In my interpretation, I view the hills as a place to heal. During trauma, loss, or distress, create a hill. My 'hill' is my faith which I focus on to heal.

What hill will you focus on to help you heal?

_____

_____

_____

_____

_____

_____

_____

Beyond the Abyss

Grief, trauma, or loss can lead one down a deep, dark and seemingly bottomless pit, pulling you into the unknown, a place of darkness where you may feel far away from the light.

While you are healing, you may feel far away from the light. When people are in a dark place, they often think it is negative or bad. When thinking of darkness, one assumes there needs to be a presence of light for it to be a good or pleasant experience. But in retrospect, darkness is necessary to produce a picture. For example, after losing my mother, I sat in the kitchen and felt like I was in a dark place. I felt like I was alone and was uncertain of my existence. A dark cloud came over me and tried to settle in my heart.

Do you think there is a difference between darkness over you, darkness in you, or covering you? If so, please elaborate.

_____
_____
_____
_____
_____
_____
_____
_____

I sat there in distress, and it felt like the world was standing still. Then, as I respected my process, I understood that I would not allow what was normal to become a place of destruction. It was ok to grieve and acknowledge what I was feeling. It was ok not to be ok because I knew that I would be ok again one day.

Sometimes people think acknowledging their feelings or emotions is negative and needs to be immediately dismissed. Have you ever been around someone about to cry because of something they were sharing, and they immediately began to tell a joke or wipe their tears away? We have emotions, and we can embrace what we are feeling and then appropriately proportion them. We do this by acknowledging them, facing them, dealing with them, and not allowing them to hover over us and create arenas of storms and devastation. Don't let your dark place keep you in the dark space.

Can you think of a time when you were in a dark place in your life? Explain how that felt.

_____
_____
_____
_____
_____
_____
_____

Darkness - what good comes out of darkness? Movies, pictures, romance, and good rest. People can watch movies in a dark place - it's hard to see the screen if there is too much light. You can see stars in the sky at night; you cannot see them during the day. I have an aunt looking for black-out curtains because she sleeps better when the light isn't breaking through. In the bedroom! Yes, I said the bedroom. Some couples unite in the darkness and make love. Some of your children were made in that dark bedroom. Precious memories, I hope. Photographers go into a dark room to develop pictures. Allow what you are going through to develop you. It may be dark, but "picture" yourself, happy again, living and learning to refocus and live in your new norm.

After reading this chapter, can you visualize your dark place more productively? If so, how?

_____

_____

_____

_____

_____

How Should I Feel?

I have heard people ask other individuals how they should feel. That question is for the person to identify how they feel, recognize it and come clean. Here are a couple of questions to help: How do you feel? Do you feel lonely? Do you feel abandoned? Do you feel useless? Do you feel forgotten? Do you feel rejected? Do you feel angry? Do you feel bitter? Do you feel overwhelmed? Do you feel at peace?

What do you feel?

_____

_____

_____

What makes you unable to identify your feelings?

_____

_____

_____

_____

What makes you avoid your true feelings?

_____

_____

_____

Sometimes we are faced with the fear of not knowing what will happen when we truly allow ourselves to open up.

What are some of the reasons you feel resistant to opening up about your feelings?

_____

_____

_____

_____

When people ask how you are doing, it is easy to reply with a positive comment: " I'm fine, fair for a square, doing amazing, too blessed to be stressed, peachy," or something very far from the truth.

What do you generally say when people ask you how you feel? Of course, some of you may say it depends on who asks, but what do you say more often than not?

_____

_____

_____

_____

Or how about when people diagnose how you feel when they look at you and say, "You must be tired," or, "Did you have a hard day?" It could be your feet are killing you, and you want them to finish talking so you can sit down. People will often tell you how you should feel, and we feed into it.

Not only feeding into it, what about the feelings we seem to merge with what others are feeling? If someone has experienced racial tension, those feelings may transpose on us, but do you really feel that, is that coming from your emotional well or someone else's?

Can you think of a time when you felt what someone else was feeling and carried it as your own?

_____

_____

_____

_____

_____

_____

_____

_____

It can also be difficult to lose someone and then lose other family members or friends to the aftermath of what happened. It is so unfortunate when families fall apart after a loss, and now you are faced with how should I feel about that? It can feel like a double loss, which can create additional pain and suffering.

Can you think of a time when you had a double loss? How did you feel and react to that?

_____

_____

_____

_____

_____

_____

Coming clean is not always easy. When I think of this, I visualize an oven. If you are like me and neglect cleaning it frequently, you will notice the food that has spilled has accumulated a buildup. Even if you are not like me, I am sure you have seen an oven like mine. Cleaning an oven after food has been baked repeatedly can be challenging to identify- what happened or what fell out of the container? Similarly, spilled emotions or feelings can be difficult to identify and deal with. We anticipate others will ask us if we are going to clean that when the real question should be, do I want to clean that?

What emotions and feelings have you allowed to build up in your life? Again, this is how you feel.

_____
_____
_____
_____
_____
_____
_____

Facing the dirty oven requires figuring out what needs to happen to get it back to its original state. Products can be purchased that require you to spray, turn on the oven and let it sit for a while. Sometimes we have to sit for a while after we begin to process what we feel.

Is there something you need to ponder in order to process how you feel?

_____
_____

_____

_____

_____

How can you begin to come clean and determine what you
are really feeling?

_____

_____

_____

_____

_____

_____

Crown and Power

I love watching movies about the late Princess Diana, and I was deeply moved when I noticed Prince William and Prince Harry walking behind their mother's casket with little emotion. During one documentary, the narrator said that although they were children, they had to display a specific type of honor because of their royal position. As a woman of power, I know about hidden tears that tend to roll out of our eyes, down our noses, and onto pillows in late-night hours. I hope they are able to express their pain despite their positions.

As one in power, a CEO, president, mayor, or community influencer, do what works for you. Whether out in the open or behind closed doors, let it out. Cry, scream, holler, dance - allow yourself to let go. It is for you. You are strong, but you are still human.

Think of the strength a dam must have in order to contain water, endure the vigor of elements, and withstand the pressure of the wind. What would happen if too much force was applied? It would burst because there is a weight capacity or limit! Everyone has a breaking point, even if you are a person of authority, president, priest, pastor, superintendent, counselor, lawyer, judge, administrator, coach, professor, doctor, scholar, athlete, leader, parent, or someone who holds a prestigious title. Just like a dam, if too much weight is applied while maintaining your operational obligations, you can find yourself overtaken and rupture under the pressure. No matter the stance or position, no matter the crown or glory, we can only carry the load for so long.

Please elaborate on a time your dam was about to burst

_____
_____
_____
_____
_____
_____
_____
_____

Explain a time when your dam did burst.

_____
_____
_____
_____
_____
_____
_____
_____

What were the results, repercussions, or consequences?

_____
_____

_____

_____

_____

_____

_____

_____

If you are unsure of what will happen when your emotional dam is released, allow someone you trust to be present as you release. If you need a doctor with you during this release due to medical conditions or other reasons, please, by all means, set up an appointment. I encourage you to go deep. I know it may be painful. That is why many individuals choose to sweep their feelings under the rug. The thought of it will allow the pain to resurface. It is ok to take your moment and not let your moment overtake you. The feelings are yours, so own them.

What are you feeling right now?

_____

_____

_____

_____

_____

_____

_____

_____

Has your position, title or dignitary stance stopped you from expressing how you really feel?

_____

_____

_____

_____

_____

If you could create a perfect stage to express your feelings, what would it look like?

_____

_____

_____

_____

_____

_____

_____

_____

_____

_____

_____

Reenact the stage you create and go for it - express yourself. You deserve it. No one is watching, and if they are, you trust them to be there. Allow someone to hug you. I never heard of a healthy hug killing anyone.

Feelings are real. Pretending as if they aren't there because of your status or who you think you need to be strong for will not help. Masquerades are for balls; you are not at a special event, or maybe you are -- a special event to unmask your pain and go forth.

Start writing down how you feel. If you can't think of the word, think of an analogy (example: I feel like a volcano waiting to explode, which can be identified as anger: Identify your honest feelings.)

_____
_____
_____
_____
_____
_____
_____
_____
_____
_____

What's in the Closet

"Out of sight out of mind" is a quote many people use to dismiss a thought, event, or individual. Just like grief, trauma, or loss, a person may believe that if they move it to the back of their mind, it will no longer exist or reside in their thought process. In order to forget the pain and move on, they want to dismiss the notion and render it powerless.

They may even push the pain so far back in their minds they don't even remember what happened or caused them so much turmoil. For example, I was looking at a bin, and it was full of stuff that once was utilized but was placed in the closet. I went into the closet; way in the back is where the bin was stored. There was so much in it that the lid could not be closed. I recall the day when I put everything in there. I was rushing to clean and put things up so no one could see them.

Often, people will have experienced situations and want to hurry up and store them in the back of the closet (their mind), so no one can see it, even them.

Can you think of what you have stored in the back of your closet (mind)?

_____
_____
_____
_____

Sometimes so much has been stored away that a person can't obtain closure or let things go. Some even think if it's out of sight, it is out of mind.

Do you primarily consider yourself a stuffer or a sorter?

_____

_____

Name a time when you found yourself as a stuffer or sorter?

_____

_____

_____

Have you ever had on a jacket that was too tight, and once you moved a certain way, it popped open, and things were exposed? You can find yourself in the same predicament by trying to stuff your emotions inside. Something can trigger the thought, and just like the jacket, it can pop, and you will be exposed and unable to control what you do or say.

How do you deal with the stuff in your bin in the back of your closet? First, begin to sort it out and deal with it. You may have to deal with one thing at a time so it doesn't become overwhelming. Next, select something you want to deal with and address it. When I think of addressing something, I imagine a letter being mailed. To send it where it needs to go, you must place an address on it. Address and confront your problem. You may be able to deal with it in one day, or it may take weeks or even months. Make a conscious effort to deal with what is in the bin so you can adequately place things where they belong.

After getting the bin out of the closet and sorting through it, I noticed all the other stuff. That's another reason we don't want to go in that closet or that junk drawer because so much was thrown in there. We understand it will take time to get it cleaned out. I didn't want to, but I had to. Sometimes, we don't want to go in that closet, but we know eventually we must.

This task was going to be big, so I took a deep breath, mentally prepared myself, and called for help. First, I had to have someone help me remove things and clean them out. We had to throw so much away. It was unbelievable how much trash (stuff I didn't need or no longer wanted) and out-of-date material had accumulated over time. In our lives, we throw our thoughts, emotions, pains, and disappointments in a closet and slam the door, hoping it won't pop back open.

Our lives can become so jam-packed. We don't want to look at it, so we keep the door closed, with a lock and key. We don't want people knowing what we are feeling or holding in, so we make sure no one has access to it but us. As a result, no one knows what really happened, the hurt, resentment, death, dreams, regrets, and the emotional volcano on the inside. It is your year; go for it, let it out and let it drain. If it's too much to handle, call or make an appointment with someone who can assist with helping you sort through your closet. Some things will need to be thrown out of your life because they are no good for you.

Can you think of something or someone who has been holding up a parking space in your mind and you are ready to tow?

_____
_____
_____
_____
_____
_____
_____
_____

Figure out what you can deal with or what feeling you have bogged down. Sometimes it is easier to recognize what doesn't need to occupy a specific space in your life anymore. We lose certain things and keep trying to replicate them or clone them. We need to drain some feelings and emotions and let go of them. We need to simply throw them away. Some of you may have gotten offended and feel this was directed towards the loved one you lost. It was not directed at any particular person or thing but at what is in your closet. I am asking you to look in your closet. Is there anything you know you need to throw away? If your answer is yes, keep reading. How you ask? You can tell yourself that chapter of your life is closed, then permit yourself to move on without that job, position, connection, or relationship. If you lose a loved one, you will not see them again, but they will always be in your heart. Be reassured, and you can go back to the previous chapters of your life and think of the good times you shared.

It took days for us to clear out my closet. Once we organized everything, I labeled the bins and put things where they belonged. Once you sort through it, labeling things will allow you to see what you have accomplished. The closet will pop open when trauma hits and past circumstances haven't been dealt with. When you have dealt with experiences, you will be able to look in the closet and say, I overcame that, I sorted that out, or I dealt with that. You can begin to understand what you need to do or have an idea of how you can move on or bounce back.

Bounce Back Game

Have you ever thrown a ball against the wall and wanted it to bounce back to you? It becomes even more challenging when the ball has no air. Life will knock the wind out of you, and you can find yourself stuck with no motivation, will, or desire to progress or move forward.

Can you think of a time you felt like situations knocked the life out of you?

_____
_____
_____
_____
_____
_____
_____

Get your air back! How? Again, recognize where you are and identify what you need. Don't expect people to know what you need or hope they give you what you lack. You must be mindful of what will help you heal and bounce back. Your friends and family may be there for you but may not be able to provide you with what you need. Create a bounce-back list. What does that look like for you?

Check off what would work for you.

- o   Vacation
- o   Staycation

- Time to laugh
- Someone to talk to
- Someone to comfort you with touch
- Someone to encourage you
- A massage
- Exercise
- Go to dinner
- Get a pedicure/manicure
- Words of affirmation
- Go watch a movie
- Place of tranquility
- Reassurance
- Hobby
- Plan an event
- A safe place to talk without ridicule
- A nice meal
- Someone to offer advice
- Go Fund Me account
- Intimacy
- Going back to college
- Cultivating yourself
- Eating healthier
- Going to church or your place of worship
- Starting a business
- Focusing on what you need
- Writing a book

How can you release yourself or gain the air back so you can bounce back?

_____

_____

_____

_____

_____

_____

_____

_____

_____

_____

_____

What Season is This?

We understand environmental seasons and can recognize how to adapt. For example, in the winter, you dress to stay warm. In the fall, you are in a transition. In the summer, you dress to keep cool and prepare for new beginnings in the spring.

When people experience trauma or loss, they may be in a season of disbelief or even experiencing a state of shock. Since your loss or trauma, have you found yourself having anxiety or panic attacks, experiencing fear, anger, irritability, obsessions and compulsions, emotional numbing and detachment, depression, shame, or guilt? If so, that is a part of the psychological reaction.

Many people look for citations and sources for information to give credit to, but you won't find a lot of that in this book. Instead, I am expounding upon my experiences, pain, sweat, and tears. The seasons I endured and now the oil from my traumas and losses are being poured out to you in hopes of being a healing ointment of hope. I am not claiming to be a doctor or recommending treatment, but this book is an avenue for you to reflect upon or consider the information I am presenting. Everyone's experiences are different, but one thing about loss is most individuals who face it feel some pain. Mine is from personal experiences, and I am becoming transparent. I have walked alongside many individuals who have gone through trauma during various seasons of their lives. I understand how support and consistency have been instrumental in their healing.

Earlier in the book, the man standing at the coffin was Apostle Charles Howard, my husband, and I was the woman encouraging him to cry. I lost a covenant son, and it was his biological son, Charles Howard Jr. Several months after his passing, people expressed their concern about how my prayers were different before he passed and how my spiritual petitions seemed to lack the passion they once had when I used to pray. That was the moment I truly understood that some people do not understand grief and how we all will encounter seasons where we have to adapt to the emotional environment around us at that time. Likewise, I realized some people don't know how to maneuver or accept those in their season of grief.

After losing my covenant son, I went into a place where I had to adapt to a new norm. Sometimes people find it difficult to talk about grief or even mention the individual's name or events you once shared. Yet, believe it or not, talking about the person can be a form of healing associated with discussing the memories and things about them that made you laugh or smile.

After the loss, I didn't speak to people for months because I was trying to get through that tough and challenging time. This was all new, and I was trying to figure out where to place these emotions and deal with the tidal wave of pain. I went through a quiet season, shall I say, my fall season, and some people did fall off. If people fall off in your life, you keep holding on. People may try to find many ways to help you deal with the grief during your season of transition. Sometimes they do not know how to do it effectively. I try to be very sensitive and careful with what I say and how I respond to people, but it's only because I am familiar with that season. We all may respond or "dress" differently, but the pain is common. People sometimes say things that don't make sense, such as - How do you feel? Or articulate other phrases to try to decrease the pain.

In some cases, it doesn't feel like comfort, but a knife or a dagger that digs deeper into the inside of you. I have found myself in error telling someone Merry Christmas or Good Morning, and they had just lost someone dear. They said there's nothing merry or good about this. I immediately apologized for my attempt to comfort.

Can you think of a time when someone tried to offer you comfort but brought you pain? What did they say, how did they say it, or what did they do?

_____
_____
_____
_____
_____
_____
_____
_____
_____

You may be in disbelief and shock, but know you are not alone during this challenging time. So, dress for the season you are in and work towards entering your summer season one day.

Cinderella's Shoe

We are all familiar with the famous Cinderella story and how many tried to fit the royal slipper in the hope of winning the prince's heart.

Many experts, family members, and friends run to the rescue or extend advice in an attempt to provide what they think we need. Yet, it boggles me how some individuals giving advice have never walked down the road you are on.

Can you elaborate on a time when someone tried to give you comfort or information about something they didn't know anything about?

_____
_____
_____
_____
_____
_____
_____
_____

In the midst of my transition, people would try to "send" a sense of ease, but it wasn't working as effectively for me. It is ok to let people know what you need when going through trauma or loss. Sometimes we won't know what we need, or articulate the intensity of what we have gone through. This is an important element for people to understand.

There are times when it is good to be quiet and LISTEN. People grapple for words to send relief, but they can be daunting and unknowingly insensitive in some cases. I say unknowingly because people will say, "I understand" or "I know how you feel." However, they still have their mother, father, covenant son, dream job, home, spouse, children, limbs, security, job, marriage, or whatever they still possess, and you don't. They simply can't know what it is like to walk in your shoes.

Find a group that can support you in what you are going through. Google the local groups you are searching for in your surrounding area. Contact your local community resource agency or ask your counselor if they are aware of places to direct you. There is a Cinderella out there who has the same shoe as you.

Screaming Teapot

At times, I wish we were like a teapot. Teapots release a noise to let you know the water is ready. So many times, people want to hold on to their pain because they feel they deserve it. But they don't know how to release it, who to release it to, or when they are ready to release it at all.

In addition to feeling like you can't get over the pain, you feel like you won't ever be able to rid yourself of the excruciating agony. This agony resides inside, and you can sometimes convince yourself that it will never go away.

I didn't rush time and allowed it to heal some of the pain. These are some of the things I did during my time of trauma, grief, and loss, and I would like you to consider incorporating these productive and stress-relieving strategies:

Pray meditate

Join a grief support group

Contact local hospitals and other local organizations for resources or groups related to trauma, grief, and hardships.

Walk

Ride a bike

Eat healthily

Eat stress-relieving foods (Watch out for foods high in fat and sugar-chocolate was my downfall.)

Talk about how you feel

Travel

Laugh (when trauma or grief hits, nothing is funny or comical, so I found a comedy show or a movie that made me laugh); laughter can be healing.

Dress up for no reason (compliments uplift, and if no one gives you one, give yourself one)

Get a makeover (some makeup counters will give you a complimentary one; remember to call in advance)

Get your hair done or hair cut

Buy a new hairstyle (for those who don't know what that is, get a wig)

Go dancing

Go to an exercise class

Read an encouraging book

Watch an uplifting series (It will give you something to look forward to)

Reminisce on the good days and experiences

Do something you have always wanted to do but didn't have the nerves (check with your health care physician first: go skating, do pottery, try a creative sport, play kickball - be careful not to injure yourself)

Which of these things will you consider doing?

_____
_____
_____
_____
_____
_____
_____

If not listed, what is something you can do?

_____
_____
_____
_____
_____
_____
_____

Don't hide behind what you feel. Instead, let it resurface, acknowledge it and take your moment. (Deep breathing helped me! Every time I thought of my loved one or the situation, I would breathe and release- the balloon.)

Many of these activities helped me deal with trauma, grief, and loss in a healthy manner. Of course, I cried when

I needed to cry. But I did not allow myself or people to make me feel guilty for moments of happiness peeking through my window. It's ok to have a good day! You will have plenty of days that seem gloomy, so when the sunshine breaks through, permit yourself to enjoy the rays.

Even if you feel alone, know you have three people always with you. I realized who those three people were in my life: me, myself, and I. When I couldn't make it, even with myself and I, I relied on my higher power, my Lord and Savior, Jesus Christ. I allowed Him to be my strength. I know I am a strong woman, but I gained a new key through all of this.

Key: IT'S OK NOT TO BE OK BECAUSE ONE DAY YOU KNOW YOU ARE GOING TO BE OK- OK!

IT'S OK TO CRY

C.R.Y (**C**ontinually **R**elease **Y**ourself)

Do you feel better when you cry?

If you don't cry, what are some reasons why not?

_____
_____
_____
_____

It's ok to cry. It's ok not to be ok. Is your teapot telling you it's time?

Who Spilled It?

In addition to tears flowing, guess what else flows? A teapot when it is left on the stove too long. The water boils over, and then the blame game starts. Who left the teapot on the stove? One of the most enlightening experiences was the first year not having my mother for her birthday. Her birthday was November 1st, and she passed in January 2021. I had to brace myself for three months for an emotional domino effect, starting with her birthday. My mother's birthday was followed by my aunt's birthday on November 2nd, who passed the following month after my mother, to the first Thanksgiving, Christmas, and New Year without my mother. The following month, January, would not be any easier as it was her first anniversary of being gone. I was like that teapot whistling for relief and wondering who was responsible for the spillover.

I was on the phone talking to someone, and the whistling sound began ringing so loud I wanted to know who to blame. It was my first year without my mom, and I had pent-up emotions that I was trying to contain but was ready to release if they came. Sure enough, they came, but I didn't know where they were coming from. Did the person I was on the phone with knock something over? Wow, this was a new feeling, and I didn't know whether to own it or throw it like a hot potato on the person I was talking to. This new experience was so strange; I told the person I would call them back.

I didn't want to blame the teapot on them, but they were the closest ones to me during my expressive encounter at the time. As I thought about my mother, her life, her birthday, and her passing, I was slightly overwhelmed because not only did I have to deal with losing her, but other traumatic experiences that I was not prepared for nor would have ever anticipated from her passing. In this chapter, I want to make people aware there may be an after spill or a spill-over during trauma or grief. If you don't deal with the screaming teapot, you may transpose your feelings or emotions on an innocent bystander and blame them for not taking the pot off the stove or turning the stove off. When you are uncertain, it may be beneficial to step back and assess the situation. After I stepped back for a day, I realized it was me and my feelings that were spilling over. Oh my, this was new, and I realized that not only could I hear the teapot whistling, but what I was feeling had spilled over. I realized I needed to be prepared to repeat previous steps and reintroduce strategies when dealing with grief, trauma, and loss. Wow, was everything I carefully and strategically released and let go of resurfacing? How did I end up here? What the what? I didn't think that was possible. During this ordeal, I learned those were not old emotions but new ones intensified by the feelings, pinnacle events, and anniversary dates. These things were combined. Although I tried so hard to brace myself for my mother's birthday and other events, it hit with a hard impact. Like a car accident, when a person braces for what they see coming, they may sustain more injuries.

After I recognized what was occurring, I took some time to grieve, prayed, took a walk, obtained a good night's rest, talked to somebody, determined my emotional forecast, and took time to see myself and where I was mentally and emotionally. I ended right back at grief's door, but I wasn't going to knock or go in. I acknowledged it, allowed myself to feel it, processed it, and after a while, I moved on. After acknowledging I was the teapot that spilled over, I needed to make things right after receiving my new revelation. I had to ask myself, was I letting my steam off on an innocent person who cared about me? They gave me my space, and during that time, I pondered what I was feeling and how this newfound experience affected me.

Once I processed where I was and landed back in a healthy space, I reached out to them because an apology was necessary. I recognized that I expected someone to fill an emotional space I needed to get rid of. Isn't it something how we desire people to join us where we are even if we don't need to be there? Have you ever been with a person who was depressed and wanted you to join them? Have you ever been with an angry person who was upset because they couldn't alter your attitude to line up with theirs?

During this experience, I have learned to take the time to process what I need to process. I also have learned to talk to individuals close to me and advise them of upcoming anniversaries or events that can cause emotional triggers. I will explain to them in advance what may be occurring and ask them to be patient with me if I respond differently than usual. Please note this doesn't give me or anyone else a license to run people over, but it should indicate this may be a good time for people in your life to move out of the way.

When the teapot is whistling, figure out why? Don't start blaming people for the spill because it very well may be you. Instead, take advantage of your mental health exercises and prepare for your mental forecast. If you know it consists of thunderstorms, then stay inside; if you know it is raining, take an umbrella. Prepare yourself and use Bounty as an example. If an emotional spill happens, be prepared to quickly pick it up, keep moving forward, and 'Respect Your Process.'

Can you think of a time when someone spilled their emotions over on you?

_____
_____
_____
_____
_____
_____
_____
_____
_____
_____

Can you think of a time when you spilled your emotions on someone else?

_____

_____

_____

_____

_____

_____

_____

_____

Like a fire escape, come up with a plan you can use if you have an upcoming emotional trigger. This will prevent you from spilling over or prevent your spill from affecting others.

Respect Your Process

Have you heard these sayings? – "Get over it." – "It's time to move on." – "I know what you are going through."

How did you react when these statements were made?

_____

_____

_____

_____

_____

Quiet the noises around you to identify what you are going through. Process where you are emotionally and what you are experiencing internally. Don't allow what you are feeling to kill you internally. How do you do this? Sit and ask yourself what you are feeling. Sometimes people use a feeling chart with various emotions to determine what they are dealing with. There will be times when so much is going on that you honestly can't identify it because several emotions are playing tag.

Is there a time when your emotions were playing tag? If so explain

_____

_____

_____

_____

_____

So, join the game. When a feeling comes, please write it down on your phone, a tablet, or journal it. Catch your thoughts and emotions while they are present. Example: If you are angry, record it on your phone (make sure you have enough data). Start talking about how you feel and why you feel that way. Don't try to make sense of it. Keep talking until you run out of what to say. In some instances, you can reveal what you feel because others may not identify it or know how to give you what you are searching for.

While respecting your process, you may feel like you are on a roller coaster. You will have up days and down days. If you have ever ridden a roller coaster, you realize that once the bars lock and the ride begins, it cannot stop midway to let you off.

Can you think of a situation you were in that felt like a roller coaster ride? If so explain

_____
_____
_____
_____
_____
_____
_____

You're going up the roller coaster thinking about many different things. "I'm afraid! I want to get off!" Tears may come, you may feel like you're getting ready to die, your stomach may be full of anxieties, and you realize at that point there's no turning back.

You're on the ride of your life, going up and down, being tossed upside down, and this ride will continue until you reach the end.

On the roller coaster of grief, trauma, or loss, decide how you deal with the unexpected emotions?

_____

_____

_____

_____

_____

_____

_____

The feelings may come from not wanting to continue or going into a cave all by yourself.

The good thing about a roller coaster is it must come to an end. Be reassured that one day it will get better. Think positive! See your rainbow at the end of the storm! Know that your life jacket will work, and you will resurface. Embrace the idea that brighter days are coming. Visualize the sun shining. Speak to yourself and declare something good will come. Recognize you deserve to live life to the fullest. Encourage yourself and look forward to the next chapter of your life. You deserve joy in your life.

Think of something you look forward to

_____

_____

_____

_____

Write something to encourage yourself

_____

_____

_____

_____

_____

_____

During the transition, I learned to respect my process. I realized that everyone would not understand or comprehend how I dealt with the grief. Everyone has their way of dealing with it. Some people want to ignore it, and others want to address it head-on, while others will simply move on and act as if it has not happened. I am sort of afraid for individuals who handle grief in that manner because if you don't deal with it now, you will have to deal with it later.

How do you deal with grief, trauma or loss?

_____

_____

_____

_____

_____

_____

What are some things you need to deal with?

_____

_____

_____

_____

_____

_____

_____

_____

_____

Rebuilding After the Fall

When I think of "tumbling down," I think of Humpty Dumpty, 911, and the building collapse in Florida in 2021. People were sleeping and living their lives, not expecting it to be their last day. Rescue teams immediately began to try to salvage what they could. It took teams of people from organizations who worked tirelessly to save people. Time was against them.

Can you think of a situation when you felt like time was against you?

_____

_____

_____

_____

_____

_____

_____

I have realized that some people don't want to deal with their pain. They would rather walk away from the scene of collapsed hopes, dreams, loss of loved ones, or the reality of facing whatever was presented or deleted from their lives. So the number one remedy for some is to "not deal," walk away from it, act as if nothing has happened, be so numb that you can't face it, or self-medicate.

Can you elaborate on a time when you walked away after something collapsed?

_____

_____

_____

_____

_____

_____

_____

I admit I had to take a moment to regroup and allow my wounds to heal. I needed to strengthen the skin that I was in. I was fragile and needed to regain my strength.

Explain a time when you felt fragile

_____

_____

_____

_____

_____

_____

_____

When a person walks away, you walk further away from dealing with it. The further a person walks away from it, they think that it no longer exists, but something may happen in life and trigger what you thought was far away in your past. I always tell my kids, "If you don't deal with it now, it will deal with you later." Later will come. You may have to go back and rehash through the debris of what fell months ago, years ago, or a century ago. Walking away doesn't mean it didn't happen. It just means that it will still be there. So often, we want people to deal with the collapsed structure. But, even if they do, it won't take away what we lose or feel after the fall.

If you go through the debris of things, you walked away from, what would you find?

_____
_____
_____
_____
_____
_____
_____
_____
_____
_____

In some cases, it could prolong the healing. For example, some people feel that working a lot or remaining occupied can take the pain away, but it can surprise you when you trip over a brick that was supposed to be in your past. And then that brick becomes a trail that leads you back to your pain.

Looking at the debris can be overwhelming but find a team to help you: a friend, your pastor, your partner, your colleague, a counselor, or a therapist. Sometimes the therapist may prescribe you something to help you deal with the initial pain.

Who can you ask to be on your team?

_____
_____
_____
_____
_____

The thought of not knowing how you will overcome it can be draining.

How do you replenish yourself when you feel drained?

_____
_____
_____
_____
_____
_____
_____

On top of being exhausted from working through the debris, you may still be challenged with understanding and working through the complexity of your grief, trauma, or loss. All of this can suck the very life out of you and feel like a constant leech zapping your stamina and zeal to live. Thinking of all you have lost can be traumatizing within itself. Losing your memory, losing loved ones or friends because of who you decide to be with, or for your decisions regarding religion or politics. Being unable to connect with family members due to incarceration.

Disconnected for those who are in mental facilities or nursing homes. Being isolated and depressed due to aging and feeling your body has let you down. Being eased out and marginalized. Feeling hopeless because of a relationship severed due to the influences of other Individuals or circumstances. Not being able to see people you cherish ever again due to a drug overdose or being murdered. So much going down the drain can be exhausting.

What or whom have you lost that has caused you to feel lifeless?

_____

_____

_____

_____

_____

_____

_____

What have you done, or what can you do to begin to rebuild or gain strength to move on?

_____

_____

_____

_____

_____

_____

Facing that mountain or molehill of pain and determining how to position it in your life to help you advance takes courage, determination, acceptance, and motivation. I am hoping you can look your situation in the face and tell it, "Giant, you must fall." I am writing these words to empower and walk alongside you, to see yourself equipped with a slingshot to knock down any gigantic obstacles of emotion or doubt, feelings of failure or self-pity standing in your way. Loosen up your bootstraps or put on your big person clothes and move toward it. Don't run away or resent dealing with it. You got this.

What strengths or attributes do you have to help you begin to restore? Don't say nothing. You are powerful, find your inner light switch and turn it on.

_____
_____
_____
_____
_____
_____
_____
_____
_____
_____
_____
_____

If you use all your energy to dread something, it can drag it out, but you can make the time go faster when you decide to face it and use your energy to rebuild.

It is important to take time out of your day to grieve, but don't allow it to ruin your entire day. I repeat, go ahead and take a moment but don't let the moment take you. Do something that you love. After I lost my mother, I planned an event, and it helped occupy my mind positively and productively. It wasn't clogged with negatively. God wants to extend His blessings unto us, but just like a faucet, if it becomes clogged with our doubt and our fear, the water will not flow appropriately, and things can get backed up. So don't let your blessings get backed up because you are unwilling to move forward.

What has clogged you?

_____
_____
_____
_____
_____
_____
_____

What can you do to unclog the clog?

_____
_____
_____

_____

_____

_____

_____

_____

Instead of focusing on what happened, take a moment to zoom in on what IS happening. Then, begin to be grateful for the memories and time shared.

Some people may feel buried underneath all the stuff and can't breathe.

What do you feel you are buried underneath?

_____

_____

_____

_____

_____

_____

_____

But the pinnacle word here is 'breathe.' If you are still breathing, you are alive. You may feel dead or even want to be removed from this earth, but you are here. You are alive to face another moment, face another day. Sometimes you need to take it day by day. Other times, you will need to take it minute by minute, and in some instances, you have to take it second by second, but no matter what, you are alive and breathing.

After experiencing pain, you may feel disconnected or as if you are in a maze. Not knowing what to do, what to say, how to feel, who to trust, how to rebuild, or how to get out can be extremely overwhelming. Instead of trying to navigate through the web of the unknown, take a moment and pause. Don't concentrate on moving or trying to figure things out. Instead, take time to regroup, redirect your thoughts, and gain strength.

Can you think of a time you felt paralyzed emotionally?

_____

_____

_____

_____

_____

_____

_____

Yes, life may have dealt you cards you didn't ask for! Yes, you may have experienced devastation, and yes, you may have experienced grief, but I challenge you to break through those stones that tried to bury you and say, "I shall arise. I shall get up and face another day." I don't know what tomorrow holds, but I know at this moment, the heavens, the galaxy, and your higher power are fighting for you. You can win. You may seem out of the race and think you will never recover, but your second wind is coming back. Feel the energy coming, your strength returning, and wings growing in your back. I am cheering you on. I know what it is to feel like a failure, so consumed with what you have lost that you forget what you still have.

Think of what you have and write them down. Let your mind and fingers work together quickly and list as many as you can.

_____
_____
_____
_____
_____
_____
_____

To be underneath the weight of devastation and heartache, at times, it feels your heart will stop, collapse or burst. You may feel like you have lost it all. You may have been rejected, dismissed, not acknowledged, and broken into pieces.

You may feel paralyzed, unable to move, or devastated, but take hope in knowing that weeping may fill your eyes, and an uncontrollable feeling may grip your being, but hold on, there will be a sunrise, and there will be a new day.
Respect your Process!

About the Author

Valerie Overton Howard is the wife of Apostle Charles Howard, mother of six adult children (five living and covenant son, Charles Howard, Jr. deceased). She is an entrepreneur, author, life coach, motivational speaker, community leader, poet, and producer who comes with a culmination of experience, knowledge, and education to empower and equip individuals. Her degree in *Nonprofit Management* has afforded her the opportunity to obtain a plethora of supervisory positions, and she is continually featured in the media. Mrs. Howard is constantly acknowledged for her ability to assist people by providing survival tools to overcome challenges related to grief, mental health, low self-esteem, poverty, suicide, family crisis, unplanned pregnancy, political barriers, drug/alcohol addictions, and other life-altering challenges. Mrs. Howard has designed diverse educational classes and workshops to address these issues. In addition, she is assigned to equip teams and leaders with the cultural wisdom and emotional intelligence needed to construct culturally inclusive and safe environments where people flourish.

Valerie Overton Howard is on the front line to initiate change and participates in productive rallies such as "Drop the Guns" and "Bring Back Our Girls," to name a few. She is a game-changer and originator of her talk show, "Valerie Overton Howard, Just Keeping it Real," The talk show provides hope while highlighting and addressing mental health, local and worldwide issues, and other sensitive topics from credible professionals and individuals' personal stories. She is the president of several organizations and has yearly events to provide knowledge and spread love and inspiration.

Valerie Overton Howard is the CEO of a Non-profit business. She has spearheaded a task force called "Joining Forces to Save Lives," She engages mental health professionals, political leaders, police officials, drug abuse counselors, and faith leaders to brainstorm and create productive solutions to meet the overwhelming demands plaguing individuals, families and the community. Mrs. Howard has many testimonials in her archives on how she has taken individuals from all walks of life from a place of desolation to a stance of wholeness by administering Individual Service Plans, facilitating workshops, and creating other avenues to assist persons of all ages in obtaining successful careers, educational diplomas and paths to propel towards their destiny. She was nominated for the "Woman of the Year" and identified as a reliable pillar in the community. Still, out of everything she has done, her greatest reward is knowing her family, who are her greatest TREASURES, call her blessed, and her name is **written in the Lambs Book of Life.**

It All Came Tumbling Down Journals are available for purchase.

Email valerieovertonhoward27@gmail.com for details or to share your experience after reading It All Came Tumbling Down.

Made in the USA
Monee, IL
08 October 2022